HOW, WHEN, AND WHERE
TO GO PUBLIC WITH A SMALL COMPANY

How, When, and Where to Go Public With a Small Company

E. Wilson Roberts

An Exposition-Banner Book

Exposition Press   New York

EXPOSITION PRESS, INC.

50 Jericho Turnpike, Jericho, New York 11753

FIRST EDITION

LIBRARY OF CONGRESS CATALOG CARD NUMBER: 72-94571

SBN 0-682-47648-X

Dedicated to
Sally, Ricky, Jimmy and Carolyn

Contents

Preface

Go Public! These words are magic to the owner or major stockholder of a privately-held corporation. If he has a *sound company* in a *growth industry,* he can enhance the stature of the company and, at the same time, greatly increase the value of his own holdings through a public sale of the stock.

Going public is a difficult and complex task. It requires a great deal of patience and perseverance on the part of all parties concerned. It may take as long as twelve months to get a registration effort completed, even in the case of a larger, well-known company.

For the small company, the task is even more formidable. First, it is difficult to obtain underwriting for small issues. Most of the larger investment bankers aren't interested in issues of less than $1,000,000, or in companies with net earnings of less than $250,000.

Second, even if you obtain underwriting, the lack of a national or regional image makes the sale of stock to the public more difficult than for the larger, more established firm.

But, *it can be done!* You can go public without the glamour of bigness if you have a good solid operation with a successful record. It requires more effort, a superior sales job on the part of management (selling the potential underwriter), but the result usually justifies the extra effort.

In this book, we discuss briefly the techniques of going public with special emphasis on the unique problems facing the executive of a small company wanting to sell stock in the public marketplace.

This book is not intended as a technical manual, but rather as a general guide for the small company executive in his efforts to "put the package together." It includes tips on *pitfalls to avoid,* as well as samples of actual agreements used in the registration process, and a sample underwriting agreement. In addition, it contains a glossary of terms to assist in understanding the language of the securities market.

Above all, you, as the small company manager, should not be discouraged by the sure "rebuffs" you will receive. In one instance an *underwriter* was unable to proceed on the date an issue was allowed "effective" by the SEC, and the issuer was like a "bride left at the altar." The company was forced to begin anew, but three (3) months later, the offering was successful!!

So this, in a sense, is a *rah rah* book. We've been through the process and know how discouraging and utterly frustrating it can become. Our sole purpose in attempting this work was to shed some light on what can be a dark pathway. If it in any way helps some distraught and dismayed executive facing the same problems, then it will have been worthwhile indeed!

Good reading, good luck and Godspeed!

Acknowledgments

This was a labor of love. Having been an executive of a small company attempting to go public, I know well the frustrations and disappointments of such an attempt.

Even so, most credit belongs to those persons who assist the author in his efforts. With this in mind, I gratefully acknowledge the assistance of the following persons, without whose help this book would not have been possible; Miss Julia Wilson, writer and consultant, St. Croix, U.S. Virgin Islands, who edited parts of the manuscript; Robert C. Hunt, Esquire, of the law firm of Hunt and Bell, Chattanooga, Tennessee, who offered much encouragement and assistance, and to my secretary, Mrs. Harold Trip, who painstakingly typed the manuscript—over and over again.

Thank you.

HOW, WHEN, AND WHERE
TO GO PUBLIC WITH A SMALL COMPANY

1. Why Go Public?

There has been a significant increase in public offerings in the last decade. *Why* this great influx of new issues? *Why go public? Why not?*

Simply stated, the capital requirements for growth companies today are such that funds cannot be generated internally in amounts sufficient both to satisfy the clamor by stockholders for dividends, and to maintain or acquire a competitive stance in the marketplace at the same time.

Of course, the company may be able to go to the money markets for debt capital. However, this has definite limitations. The point is soon reached where a prominence of debt capital in the balance sheet makes further borrowing very difficult unless the prior debt is repaid, resulting in a further drain on cash reserves. On the other hand, capital raised from the public sale of stock does not have to be repaid and entails no interest or debt service charges. This does not mean that "going public" is an inexpensive way to raise capital. In many cases it is not, *especially for the small company.* (We discuss the expense of a stock offering in Chapter 9).

On the other hand, conditions in the money markets are such today that it is more advantageous for the small company to attempt to sell its stock to the public. Investors seem to be more willing to take a chance on small, unknown firms than in many a year. The potential for spectacular appreciation in the value of a stock (at capital gains tax rates if, and when, realized) is evident from the past performances of stocks of relatively unknown companies.

ADVANTAGES OF A PUBLIC ISSUE

In addition to providing new capital for the company selling the stock (the issuer), there are other reasons for "going public." It is most difficult to establish a value for the stock of a privately-held corporation. A successful public offering creates a market for the stock, and creating a market establishes a value for the stock. This has many advantages. It makes *practical* the use of stock options to attract and keep key personnel. Also, a public price affords a basis for negotiations in the event of a subsequent merger or acquisition.

More important to you as the owner of a small privately-held corporation, a public underwriting can be used to enhance your own personal income and net worth. The stock of a private corporation is seldom readily marketable and, therefore, not easily valued for purposes of determining your net worth or assets. Furthermore, your holdings have virtually no liquidity, or you may be holding *restricted* or *lettered* stock (discussed in Chapter 7). Practically speaking, you are "locked-in." You cannot sell the stock, and it may not be suitable for use as collateral. Lenders are reluctant to make loans against restricted securities—particularly when the corporation is privately held. There is no market for the stock; it simply has no established value.

Going public, then, will establish a value for your holdings which can be used for a practical evaluation of your net worth for estate planning and other purposes. Your holdings become more attractive as collateral for loans with which to leverage additional investments. Even if the stock is still restricted, the public market value usually makes it more acceptable to lenders.

If you can register and sell a portion of your own holdings in the public offering, you actually free up formerly locked-in cash. This will permit you to diversify your investment portfolio and spread your risk a bit. And the circumstances are usually such that any gains realized on the sale of the stock is taxable at the capital gains rates.

Finally, because of the added influx of cash, the company is more attractive to lending institutions. The advantages of the increase in net worth due to an injection of cash from a stock sale far outweigh the disadvantage of dilution of your majority interest —*from the banker's viewpoint.* And imagine the increased growth potential through expansion, made possible by the infusion of cash.

THE DISADVANTAGES OF GOING PUBLIC

Once you decide to take your company public you open all doors and windows for public inspection. Every aspect of the company's activities become a matter of public record; nothing is sacred. If there are any "skeletons" in the closet, be assured they will not only be *found,* but they may also be *publicized* for the world to see.

When you first read the *prospectus* (or *offering circular*) you won't recognize your company. You won't believe it is in such poor condition as the prospectus will lead the prospective investor to believe. Nor will you believe the outlook for the future is so pessimistic.

Any transactions with the company, or affecting the company, must be disclosed in the registration statement. You will see such things as *your salary* in black and white (so will everyone else), and you will be embarrassed, or pleased, as the case may be! Any transactions you may have had with the company, and any disadvantages or advantages you may have obtained from such transactions, will likewise be disclosed. In short, any material fact affecting the corporation must be set forth in the registration statement.

Such full disclosure is required by law and is intended for the protection of your prospective stockholders. This is as it should be. Unsuspecting investors have often been hoodwinked by unscrupulous promoters and manipulators. Of course, the filing of a prospectus does not guarantee the success of their investment, but it does provide and disclose a certain amount of vital information on which the investor can base an opinion.

When you go public, you take on a new responsibility—to your stockholders. If the business does not continue to prosper,

you can expect to hear from them promptly, particularly if the
price of the stock slumps some after hitting the market, although
the price of your stock on the public market may have little or
no relation to the company's progress or lack of progress.

Further, you cannot run your "public" company by the "seat
of your pants" as you did when it was solely yours. You are now
responsible to a number and variety of stockholders and you must
run the company in a sound, businesslike manner. This is the
way it should have been run previously, but, of course, a privately-held corporation can be, and often is, run much more in-
formally than a public one. In any event, you will have a much
greater responsibility in dealing with your stockholders, directors,
the government and the public in general.

There will be considerable internal and external pressure to
continue the growth rate you have established. Suddenly, every
financial report you publish and every utterance you make will
take on extreme importance. If it is not better or more optimistic
than the previous one, you are in for problems, regardless of the
reasons. You will be under constant pressure from stockholders—
for the initiation of dividends or increased dividends, and about
many other things, some of which will utterly amaze you!

The public company's complete financial situation is not only
open to *public* scrutiny, it is also open to the inspection of your
employees and others. Some won't be satisfied with the amount
of money the corporation is making; some may feel you, as an
executive, are too highly paid. You will soon realize that information which was previously confidential is now available to out-
siders, including your competitors. They may be able to pick up
valuable information from your reports and financial statements,
and there's absolutely no way you can deny them access to these
facts, especially if they become stockholders in your company
themselves. *And they will!*

You, as the owner or major stockholder, of a private corporation, must think long and hard about going public. You should
carefully weigh the possible advantages and disadvantages of doing
so.

You should discuss the matter thoroughly with your attorneys, accountants and other professional advisors. It is a different ball game when you are operating in a strange, open arena, under unfamiliar ground rules. It isn't easy and it isn't always the best thing to do.

In the final analysis, *not all* companies *should* "go public," nor *can* all companies "go public."

2. Special Problems for the Small Company

It may be easy to decide that you *want* to go public. The big question will then be *can you go public? Is the company ready to go public? Will a competent underwriter think you are ready?* Will he think he can *sell* the stock? Is the public in the *mood?* Is *now* the right time?

There are no hard-and-fast answers to these questions, unfortunately. The answers depend on many variables. Take a long and *objective* (if that's possible!) look at your company.

Do you have a good record of earnings and growth of earnings? The longer this record, the better your prospects. And the better the earnings, the easier it will be to convince a prospective underwriter that he can sell your company's stock to the public.

Your financial records must indicate that you are able to maintain close control over operating expenses, and that you know where you stand at all times. This may seem obvious, but it is not always simple. Many small companies cannot, or do not maintain the kind of cost-control accounting required to produce these records. The *excuse* may be lack of personnel or the added expense, but there is no valid *reason* for not doing so.

Even though audited figures are not always required in a public offering, it is sound business to have such information. When considering a public offering, take great care in the choice of an accounting firm for audit purposes (see Chapter 6).

An equally important factor in a successful stock offering is the caliber of your management team. Not only must you have capable men at the top, but you must also have sufficient depth of management so that the loss of one person will not seriously impair the progress of the company. The team should inspire confidence in its ability to manage the affairs of the company so as to insure that the long-term prospects are bright!

This is often a problem for the very small company because it lacks the depth in management experience that larger companies can more easily acquire. Another reason for going public is that the attendant publicity and the added capital will help make the company more attractive to effective young executives, and enable you to obtain and hold them.

It will be helpful if the industry of which your company is a part is popular with investors. I was on the management team of a franchise company which went public at a time when the bloom was gone from franchise issues. In fact, franchising, in general, was in disrepute. We had to overcome adverse industry publicity in order to bring the stock to the public market, whereas just a few years before, franchise companies had been the *fad* on Wall Street.

Being in the *right industry* at the *right time* makes going public with a small company much easier. Regardless of how good your prospects are or how much money you are making, it will be difficult to go public if you are in the *wrong industry*. You must be in a *growth* industry—one whose prospects for the future are unusually bright and within which you are a dynamic, emerging factor.

The small size of your company may present problems when you are looking for an underwriter or trying to decide whether or not you are ready to go public. Usually, the larger and better-known the company, the better the chance of a successful public offering. But if all small companies waited until they became big, there would be few new issues on the market. And most would wait a long time.

It will always be more difficult for the small company executive to sell an underwriter on his stock offering. We pointed out in the preface that most underwriters prefer a company with net earnings of $250,000 or more and an offering of at least $1,000,000. Many small companies that are otherwise sound cannot meet these criteria.

The underwriter has valid reasons for not wanting to take an issue of less than $1,000,000. He has several problems with a small issue, one being the difficulty of maintaining a satisfactory *after-market* with a small volume of trading.

A second problem, especially for those firms with more than one office, is that there simply aren't enough shares available for allocation to the various offices for sale.

Another reason is simply that of profitability. Underwriters are in business to turn a profit just as you are, and the larger firms have such an overhead that the return from a small offering just isn't attractive.

In summary, the small company must have a solid record of earnings, good management, and better-than-average growth prospects before it can consider going public. Your underwriter must be reasonably assured the stock issue will be successful. He puts his name *on the line* and his reputation is at stake. He will want to visit your offices, ask questions, talk to your advisors, your employees and executives. He will generally inspect your company from every angle. You will be irritated by his incisive questions, elated by some, and embarrassed by others. However, a good underwriter will ask these questions and it is necessary that honest, forthright answers be forthcoming.

As to whether or not the public is ready to buy your stock, the underwriter is the best judge, and this decision should be left to him. He can well advise you as to the best timing for the issue.

Finally, don't overlook the obvious. The underwriter wants honest and dedicated management. He likes to see that honesty and dedication exhibited by the willingness of management to commit their own money to the business. If management is not so committed, then the underwriter may not be interested, either.

You can readily see why it is harder for the small company to swing a public offering than for a large firm to do so. The small company executive must be prepared to meet these problems with a well-prepared sales presentation. It can be done; it's being done every day; *you can do it, too!*

3. Alternatives to a Public Offering

You may, for some reason, or combination of reasons, decide not to attempt to go public by way of a registration effort, or it may develop that you are not able to sell stock to the public. Unfortunately, this will not alleviate your need for additional capital, providing, of course, you had a *bona fide* need in the first place. In this event, you will need to turn your attention to alternative methods of financing your company.

In this chapter, we will discuss several of these alternatives. In some cases, these alternatives may be simple and commonplace; others may be complex and unique. In all cases, you should consult with your professional advisors prior to making any decisions as to which method you may select.

Venture Capital Financing

Venture capital financing is that available through companies formed for the specific purpose of helping small companies that are unable to take advantage of conventional financing sources and methods. This type of financing may take the form of a loan, or loans, either long-term or short-term, or it may take the form of equity capital. Usually, these firms put money into investment situations where they can realize long-term capital gains and may seek an outright equity interest in a company. They are not normally interested in income, but rather seek potential capital growth, and in some cases, a term loan will be exchanged for an option to obtain an equity interest at a future date.

Venture-capital-financing companies may be privately or publicly owned. However, a particular group, the Small Business Investment Companies (SBIC), are chartered and licensed under federal law for the express purpose of assisting small companies. A list of these SBIC's may be obtained from any regional office of the Small Business Administration.

One of the most common causes of failure in the search for financing is the inadequacy of the *presentation* or *proposal*. Nothing *turns off* a potential investor faster than an applicant who does not have a well-prepared presentation showing how the proposed funds will be utilized. He must be assured the money is (1) needed and (2) that it will be judiciously used.

In attempting to attract venture capital financing (or any type of financing) a proposal such as outlined in Chapter 7 will be of much help. Usually these firms will be looking for the same kind of information the underwriter looks for in a public issue, the chief difference being that he is willing to take a bigger risk than is the underwriter.

The venture capital firm will make an exhaustive study of your management, financial position, product line and the prospects for future growth. If it likes what it sees, it can provide money, advice, and even managerial assistance—all three being essential ingredients to a successful operation.

The advantages of this type of financing are obvious. It provides a more-or-less permanent source of funds, but more than that, you may also obtain some excellent management assistance and/or advice along with the funds. In addition, you avoid the public exposure of a public offering of your stock.

THE SPIN-OFF

The *spin-off* is simply another method of going public. It allows a portion of the company's stock to be placed on the public market, on a trading basis, within the rules established by the Securities Act of 1933 and 1934.

Here's how it works: A new corporation is formed and acquires 100 percent of the stock of your privately-held corporation. At the same time, a portion of the stock of the new corporation is purchased by a publicly-owned corporation, which *registers* the stock and distributes it as a *dividend* to its stockholders. The key to the success of the *spin-off* is to have enough of the stock of the new corporation registered and distributed so as to allow for active trading by the public.

If the spin-off is handled properly and the appropriate registration is completed, the stock may be traded publicly. One important consideration, however, is that to create a proper market for the stock in the so-called *after market,* there must be enough broker/dealers who are interested in the stock to assist in *making a market* for it. Otherwise, the issue will be *flat* and the result will be a decline in the price of the stock.

The advantages of the spin-off technique are essentially the same as those found in the public stock offering, i.e., a value is established for the business, a market for the stock is created, and the public in general has more of an interest in the company since its stock is publicly traded.

PRIVATE PLACEMENTS

Private placements are discussed briefly in Chapter 4. If offered to a *limited number* of persons, the sale of securities to those persons may qualify for an exemption from registration under the *private placement* exemption. This exemption is available only when the SEC is satisfied that the securities are being acquired for *investment purposes* and *not for resale* or *distribution.* Usually, if the securities are held for two years the exemption will be valid. There are many limitations on the private placement exemption, and expert advice should be sought to determine if this is the proper route for you to take. It will take much time and effort on your part as the small company executive in order to consummate a private placement. This is time that can probably be better spent attending to the company's business. Therefore, it is best to work through an investment banker, underwriter, or management/financial consultant who will act as an agent in arranging the placement of your stock.

Once again, a well-prepared proposal (see Chapter 7) will be most helpful in approaching the prospective purchaser. It is best to allow your underwriter or consultant to assist in the preparation of the proposal, since he will be using it in attempting to place the issue.

An advantage of the private placement over the public offering is that it is usually completed more quickly and it is much more flexible. In addition, it is usually *less expensive*. On the other hand, you may get a lower price for your stock in a private placement than you would if you complete a public offering. In addition, there may be certain restrictions in your placement agreement that would not be found in the public offering. The prospective purchaser may seek to impose restrictive controls on your management authority, or may even seek to gain complete control, directly or indirectly, of your company. While this is not always the case, the agreement should be reviewed very carefully by you and your professional advisors.

4. The Government and Your Company

In 1933 Congress passed a Securities Act to correct certain abuses that had existed previously. Generally speaking, the Securities Act of 1933 makes it unlawful to use interstate commerce, or the mails, to offer to sell securities unless a registration statement has been filed; or to sell a security or deliver a security after sale unless a registration statement is in effect. In addition, the act requires complete disclosure of certain information so that potential investors may make an informed decision whether or not to invest in a given security.

Although the Securities Act of 1933 is very comprehensive, the Securities and Exchange Commission (SEC) does not pass upon the merit or value of the securities it reviews. It cannot advise an investor whether or not to buy; rather it determines whether the disclosures made in the registration statement and the prospectus are complete and clear enough to inform the buyer adequately. Even though the SEC may allow a registration statement to become effective, such registration does not constitute approval of the stock, nor is there certification that the statements in the registration statement are true and/or accurate.

If, after the issue is "effective," the SEC finds that the registration statement is not accurate or does not contain certain pertinent facts, it may issue a "stop order" and suspend the registration statement until it is satisfied that it has been corrected. If the inaccuracies or false statements are material, the act also provides for civil and criminal liability, and punishment therefor.

Actually, the SEC was not created under the Securities Act of 1933, but under the Securities Act of 1934, which also provided for regulation of stock exchanges, members, brokers, etc. The main office of the SEC is in Washington, D.C. There are regional offices in strategic cities located around the country. The office you deal with will depend upon the method you select in going public, and the area in which you are located.

EXEMPTIONS FROM REGISTRATION

It is possible that the sale of your stock may be *exempt* from registration under certain conditions:

PRIVATE SALE—If the sale is to be made to a specific person or is purely an isolated transaction, it may be exempt from registration, providing the buyer purchases for *investment purposes* and *not for resale*. To qualify for this exemption, offers to sell the security must be limited to a small number of people, and these "offerees" must have access to certain information concerning the issuer.

An *investment letter* is usually required to warrant, on the part of the purchaser, that he is purchasing the stock for *investment* and does not plan to resell or distribute the stock in some other way. Hence, stock purchased in this manner is called *lettered* or *restricted stock*.

Generally speaking, a purchaser of *lettered stock* must hold it for a period of not less than two (2) years before he can distribute it without arousing the suspicion of the SEC. This is a very sensitive matter and you should seek the advice of your attorney in determining whether or not your offering will constitute a *private placement* or a *public sale* of stock.

INTRASTATE ISSUE—A second exemption is the *intrastate issue* exemption. If you sell your stock exclusively within the boundaries of your own state, you may be exempt from registration. You may still be able to sell your stock to the public and save a considerable sum on registration expenses and other fees.

This is a sensitive area, however, and you should be sure that you want to use this exemption before attempting it. For instance, *a single sale* or *offer to sell* an unregistered security to an out-of-state resident can be sufficient to cause the loss of your exemption and render the entire issue illegal. Although it *may be* easier and less expensive to sell stock under the intrastate exemption, it may be very difficult to obtain underwriting for it, simply because it is *safer* for the underwriter to "go SEC."

In any event, if you go intrastate, you still must register with your own state. Therefore, you should consult with your advisors as to the advantages and disadvantages of this type registration, including the requirements of your state securities department.

A third exemption is that used most frequently by the small company; namely, *Regulation A.*

REGULATION A—If the total value of your offering is $500,000 or less, you may be eligible for the *Regulation A* exemption. We will discuss this exemption in more detail in the following chapter since it is very important to the executive of the small company. Suffice it to say that this is not truly an exemption, but is actually a *short-form registration.*

Regulation A requires an offering circular containing information similar to that found in a Prospectus. In addition, it must contain the following statement on the front page:

> These securities are offered pursuant to an exemption from registration with the United States Securities Exchange Commission. The Commission does not pass upon the merits of any securities, nor does it pass upon the accuracy or completeness of any Offering Circular or other selling literature.

Once again, your attorneys should be consulted as to the advisability of filing under Regulation A. They can also advise you as to the cost involved in registration and other fees.

There are three other exemptions to the registration requirements: (1) the dealer's exemption, (2) the brokerage transaction exemption, and (3) the exemption for certain types of securities. These are essentially *trade* exemptions, however, and we will not be concerned with them in this work, since they concern short-term notes and similar securities.

THE REGISTRATION STATEMENT

Writing the registration statement to comply with the SEC requirements will require a team effort between management, the underwriter, attorneys, and accountants.

The purpose of the registration statement is to give full and fair disclosure of facts pertaining to the securities to be offered for sale. It will include all pertinent details about the history, business and activities of the company, together with financial information. It will also include such items as names and addresses of directors, officers, and experts who prepared the statement, and will include numerous exhibits, including copies of resolutions, by-laws, charters, and other items. (It will also require copies of any sales contracts that account for more than 15 percent of your total sales).

Likewise, the prospectus or offering circular is part of the registration statement. It will include essentially the same information found in the registration statement, but will not be in such detailed form as required by the registration statement, nor will it require the exhibits.

Usually, the underwriter is in charge of writing the registration statement. However, this is not always the case and you should seek the advice of your attorney in this matter. In any event, the registration statement will contain the following:

1. a full description of corporate properties
2. an explanation of the capital structure and intended usage of proceeds from the offering
3. a description of the securities to be offered
4. financial statements
5. list of patents and copyrights
6. description of major contracts
7. description of chief products and services

In addition, all facts concerning financial dealings between the company and its officers and/or directors, including any stockholders owning 10 percent or more of the stock must be disclosed.

As mentioned previously, when you see a first draft of your registration statement, or the offering circular, you will be seized with panic. Not only is it *not* a piece of sales literature, it will be overly conservative and may even appear *negative*. It will seem designed to bring out the worst aspects of your company. Things such as your salary and the salary of your officers and directors, including all other compensations (bonuses, commissions) will be revealed, and it will contain a resume of the work history and previous employment of all your officers and directors.

Finally, the registration statement will require the signatures of all parties to the offering, including accountants, underwriters, corporate officers, directors, and any other "experts" who may have contributed to it.

THE PROSPECTUS

Even as *negative* as described above, the prospectus (or *offering circular,* in the case of a Regulation A offering), is basically the selling document for the stock issue. It is *also designed* to protect the corporation, major stockholders, directors and officers, accountants and counsel, and underwriters against liability under the Securities Act of 1933.

As mentioned previously, the prospectus contains the same basic information found in the registration statement. Since it is essentially a selling document, the information presented should be prepared in such a manner as to allow it to be read smoothly and easily. Even so, with the requirements imposed by law, it will remain primarily a negative document.

Once your registration statement has been filed, along with the prospectus and financial material, it will be reviewed by the SEC to determine whether or not the disclosures made are adequate. Obviously, sales should not be made until the SEC advises that the registration may become effective.

If the statements are found to be incomplete, the SEC will mail a *letter of comment* (sometimes referred to as *deficiency letters*) to the issuer requesting additional information, or substantiation of certain information. It is rare when the Commission will not raise any questions about the information submitted and permit the registration to become effective as originally filed.

The corrections required must be made immediately so the effective date of registration will not be delayed. When a *letter of comment* is received, all parties to the underwriting agreement should immediately get together to discuss the amendments that are required. Time is of the essence if a delay is to be avoided. Under the law, a registration statement is not effective until twenty days after the date of filing. During this period you are not allowed to sell or offer to sell stock, but a preliminary prospectus may be used during this time to acquaint the public with the issue. This preliminary prospectus is called a *Red Herring*. It is generally not complete as to the offering price, etc., and is called a Red Herring because the following legend is printed on the front in *red ink:*

> A Registration Statement relating to these securities has been filed with the Securities and Exchange Commission but has not yet become effective. Information contained herein is subject to completion or amendment. These securities may not be sold nor may offers to buy be accepted prior to the time the Registration Statement becomes effective. This Prospectus shall not constitute an offer to sell or the solicitation of an offer to buy, nor shall there be any sale of these securities in any State in which such offer, solicitation or sale would be unlawful prior to registration or qualification under the Securities Laws of any such State.

Due Diligence Meeting

Shortly before the effective date of the registration statement, a meeting should be held with the board of directors, officers, accountants and legal counsel. (Usually the underwriter and its counsel will attend.) This meeting is held for the purpose of reviewing the prospectus, line by line, and the individuals who have written or are responsible for the various portions of the prospectus are questioned as to the content of each section, and a mutual discussion regarding the section is held. This meeting is referred to as the *due diligence* or *underwrters meeting*.

Obviously, this meeting is of considerable importance. You must be able to present yourself and your associates to the members of the underwriting group as men of intelligence, integrity, sincerity, and capable leadership ability. This is, in fact, a sales meeting at which you again *sell* the underwriting group on your company.

Blue Sky Laws

In order to sell your stock in the various states, you must comply with the registration laws applicable to each state. Such security registration laws are commonly called *Blue Sky Laws*. The underwriter and your attorneys will tell you about these requirements and most likely be familiar with the various laws. Even though you may have filed a registration with the SEC, there are variations in the laws of each separate state in which you wish to sell stock and these laws must be complied with.

This is one area in which you should exercise prudence. Registration requirements in the various states can be very expensive and there is absolutely no need to qualify in a particular state unless you desire, or need, to sell stock in that state. For instance, if you are operating in a five-state area, obviously the most interest in your stock will be in that area where potential investors are familiar with your firm.

On the other hand, your underwriter may be particularly strong and have several branches in a particular state that is not included in your five-state operating area. If this is the case, he may wish you to *Blue Sky* your issue in that state. This is certainly advisable. However, you do not want to go to the expense of registering in states where there is little likelihood you will sell stock.

Some states do not require registration before the securities can be sold, but most do have some form of registration requirement. Your attorney, and the attorney for the underwriter, should advise you of the *Blue Sky requirements* in the various states.

5. Regulation A—
Is It for You?

Paragraph 3(b) of the Securities Act of 1933 authorizes the Commission to adopt rules and regulations exempting from registration security offerings that do not exceed $300,000 in amount. *This limit was raised from $300,000 to $500,000, effective in early 1971.*

Regulation A (Reg A) was issued by the SEC under this grant of authority by Congress to effect an exemption from the registration requirements of the act for smaller issues. Practically speaking, it is not an exemption at all; it is a simplified or *short-form registration.* Even so, this exemption from the general registration provisions of the Securities Act of 1933 is rather restrictive and the rules of the SEC must be complied with in all cases.

For instance, in computing the amount that can be offered under this exemption, there must be deducted from the $500,000 limitation securities sold anyone in violation of the Securities Act, i.e., selling securities without an effective registration statement. Another deduction is made for securities sold by either the issuing company or a stockholder under a Reg A offering within one year prior to the proposed offering. Further, any securities that were sold under the so-called Private Offering Exemption would have to be deducted in the event a Reg A offering was filed shortly after such a private sale.

Finally, any securities awarded as compensation to the underwriter must be included in the computation. However, if such bonus securities are placed in escrow for at least one year after the commencement of the public offering, they will not be deducted from the $500,000 limit.

The $500,000 maximum is an annual one and is available each year, even if the issue is part of a longer, overall plan, i.e.,

$2,000,000 over four years. The main advantage of Reg A is that the entire registration effort is handled at the SEC regional office. It does not have to go to the Washnigton office. Thus, the SEC staff is more accessible and convenient, and the administrative procedures usually take much less time.

Is It for You?

Going public under Reg A is probably the most attractive vehicle available to the small company. Not only is it substantially quicker than a full registration, but it paves the way for a larger, full registration effort at a later date.

Unfortunately, it may sometimes be difficult to obtain under-writing for the Reg A issue. In addition to the size problem mentioned earlier, many underwriters are simply leery of Reg A issues, a fear based on the experience of the early 1960s.

Those years saw many small, unknown companies go to the public for money on records that were somewhat less than spectacular. Electronics was the rage then and every small operator was hitting the big time. As a result, there were many collapses and much investor capital was lost in stocks of dubious quality marketed under Reg A.

Today there is still a reluctance on the part of underwriters to handle a Reg A, due in great part to these experiences. However, Reg A does seem to be making a return to prominence and the quality of those issues offered definitely makes up for the lack of quantity.

If you decide Reg A is to be your vehicle, don't be dismayed at a lack of interest on the part of some underwriters. Keep plugging until you've found one of the many houses specializing in small issues. *Smallness* is no indication of a lack of *quality* and some of these underwriters can do an outstanding job with your issue.

Filing Procedures

Upon filing notice of the registration, offering of the security can usually begin within ten days. However, as in a full registration, the regional office will generally issue a *comment letter* setting out any deficiencies they feel may exist. Practically speaking, no offer is commenced unless the SEC has concluded that no deficiencies exist, and this may require up to sixty days. Simply because your offering is filed under an exemption provided by Reg A, don't think that it necessarily means no comment letter or any lack of pertinent comments. In one particular Reg A offering, the comment letter consisted of thirteen pages. The officers of the issuer were obviously shocked and dismayed. However, the offering circular was amended promptly and the offering proceeded without undue delay.

Once the registration statement has been filed with the SEC, you will also have to qualify in the various states in which you propose to offer the securities. These Blue Sky Laws were discussed in Chapter 4.

FINANCIAL STATEMENTS

Although Reg A does not require that financial statements be certified, they must be, in fact, prepared in accordance with generally accepted accounting principles and practices. Further, most underwriters will require certification of the statements, Certified statements are advisable in any event.

The use of pro-forma statements may not be allowed unless the offering is on a *firm* underwriting basis (see Chapter 8), or in the event refunds are to be made of the subscription price if the entire issue is not sold *(all-or-none)*. A balance sheet cannot be used if more than ninety days old as of the date of the filing of notification. This time may be extended up to six months for good cause and under certain conditions. Profit-and-loss statements and statements of surplus must be for the two full fiscal years prior to the date of the balance sheet, and for any period between the close of the last fiscal year and the date of such statements.

LETTER OF COMMENT

Basically speaking, the "letter of comment" concerns changes that should be made in the offering circular, or additional information that is required. In addition, there may be questions regarding certain statements in the offering circular, and a request for clarification of certain areas of the offering circular. You may well be completely dismayed when you read the comment letter. There may be so many questions or exceptions that you are discouraged from proceeding further. However, you will find that the comment letter has a definite purpose and the SEC staff is usually very helpful in advising you of the necessary information. However, they won't write the offering circular for you. Once you have complied with the comment letter to the satisfaction of the regional office, they will term the offering "effective."

EXPENSES OF REGULATION A OFFERINGS

There is no filing fee for a Reg A offering. However, expenses for a Reg A offering are not necessarily proportionately less than those for a full registration. For instance, printing cost will vary little except as to the number of copies required and to the extent that you may not use a Red Herring. Accounting fees will basically be the same if they are certified since certification for a larger offering is not materially different from the Reg A offering. Attorneys' fees may be less, however, since the registration is not as comprehensive as a full registration effort.

The following will give you an indication of expenses to expect in a Reg A offering (excluding underwriting expenses):

Printing cost	$3,000 —	$5,000
Legal expense	3,000 —	6,000
Accounting expense	3,000 —	5,000
Miscellaneous expenses	1,000 —	2,500
Typical range of		
total expenses	$10,500 —	18,500

In summary, the public offering may well be the cheapest form of financing available to the small company, particularly in view of the amount of money raised in relation to the amount of stock sold. There are no repayment schedules to be met, nor interest to be paid!

6. Legal and Accounting

In selecting legal counsel for your offering, your regular attorney will no doubt have recommendations. Unless his is a large firm or he has prior SEC experience, he may not feel properly equipped to handle a SEC registration effort. He knows that when you begin the registration process and are working with the SEC, you should have the most qualified legal advice available. You need someone who has been through registration before and knows the intricacies of working with the SEC. It is foolish to rely upon someone who is not familiar with SEC procedures, or who is not familiar with securities offerings in general. Money spent in this manner will be money wasted.

Ask your attorney to recommend the legal firm in your area which has the best reputation for handling securities offerings. It is entirely possible there may not be an outstanding SEC firm in your city. If not, don't hesitate to go to the nearest large city and obtain the services of the best such firm available. At the same time, you should *try* to keep legal services as near to your base of operation as possible. This will result in less travel expense and lost time, because you will be in constant contact with the attorneys.

SEC legal work is very complex and highly specialized. There are serious penalties for registration statements containing misleading or false information, and you may be liable in the event your registration is not handled properly. This does not preclude your regular attorney from working on the issue, however, because there are many things he can do, and the SEC firm will no doubt recommend that he do much of the basic work.

Normally, your attorney will negotiate most of the underwriting agreement as far as technical aspects are concerned. This is especially true if you do not have someone on your management team with financial experience. On the other hand, your regular attorney will usually do much of the work in preparing the registration statement and prospectus. If recapitalization or reorganization is called for prior to the public issue, your attorney's role is most important. He must work closely with counsel for the underwriter because they will review, and approve, each other's documents. In short, the attorney is a necessary and vital link in the registration process.

In summary, get the *best!* In the long run, it will save you much money. Lost time, delays, conferences with the SEC and your directors are all very expensive. If your legal firm is experienced with securities registration, then counsel's face will be a familiar one down at the SEC office. He will receive a much better reception than someone who is not familiar with their procedures. Many times a call can save days of delay if the parties are familiar with each other and know they can rely on each other.

ACCOUNTING

You should use the same care in selecting a well-qualified accounting firm. Not only should they be expert auditors and accountants, but now they must be experienced in SEC requirements as well! You're in a new ball game with new rules to play by! A firm with SEC experience and a national or regional reputation can save you many dollars in lost time, errors, and delays. Obviously, if the financial statements are well prepared, they are better received by the SEC and the underwriters. Well-prepared financial statements by a reputable firm can materially shorten your time schedule with the SEC.

Your accountants are responsible for active participation in all financial areas of the registration statement and pospectus. They must file detailed schedules with the SEC and comply with all other rules and regulations of that agency.

If your issue is filed under the exemption of Regulation A, audited statements may not be required. However, it is always in the best interest of your issue to have the statements audited, even if not required. Of course, the prestige of a national or regional firm with SEC experience makes certification even more meaningful.

Let's face it, a *first-class* presentation will demand a *first-class* reception when it comes time for registration, and that is what you want! The facts may remain the same, but the manner in which they are presented can make a considerable difference.

7. Selecting an Underwriter

Perhaps this chapter would be more appropriately entitled "How to Get an Underwriter," for surely this will be more likely the case for most small companies. Selecting the underwriter is critical and most advice from your advisors will be to select one of the *big-name* houses.

Practically speaking, this may not be possible for the small company executive. The fact is that the large, best-known underwriters have usually established a minimum underwriting requirement of at least $1,000,000.

Therefore, your task is to select the *best available* underwriter to handle your issue, and there are *many* underwriters who will take a small issue and do an exceptionally fine job. However, they are those specializing in small issues and who have experience in handling them. An underwriter is not always easy to find and you may have to seek outside help in order to obtain public financing.

USE OF FINDERS

The small company may not have executives with the necessary experience and/or contacts to obtain underwriting for its stock issue. If this is your situation, you may want to rely on a *finder*. There is nothing wrong or illegal about this, so long as it is properly disclosed.

Finders are normally *financial* or *management consultants* who operate on a fee basis. The finder's job is to put you together with an underwriter, and usually he will want to have a hand in formulating the proposal himself. He will actually present the proposal to the financial contact, in most cases.

The finder will usually know which houses are interested in

41

your type of proposal and if he is reputable, the underwriter may well rely on his recommendations.

The issuer pays the finder, either directly or through expenses passed on by the underwriter, and the agreement with a finder should always be reduced to writing to avoid future misunderstandings. Finder's fees usually run from 3 to 15 percent of the underwriter's compensation, or ½ to 1½ percent of the total offering, depending upon the difficulty of placing the issue.

THE UNDERWRITER

Of course, you want to select a reputable underwriter. The name of such a firm on your prospectus or offering circular will make the stock even more appealing to the public investor. He will have more confidence in your stock if he sees a familiar name on the front. By *reputable,* I mean you want an underwriter with an excellent business *reputation* and one with a reputation of *handling issues similar to your own.*

You must remember that the relationship with the underwriter does not end after the initial sale of your stock. As a matter of fact, the most important time in the offering is that period immediately following the initial offering, sometimes referred to as the *after market.* During this period, the price of your stock may have a tendency to *sag* unless it was bid up over the initial offering price. Therefore, you must have an underwriter or investment banker you feel you can work with over a long period of time and rely completely upon his integrity and ability, and *one you feel will not abandon the stock after its initial offering.*

This is most important. If your stock is to be a successful and viable entry into the public marketplace, your underwriter must not only get the issue to market, but he must also be a *market maker* and enlist enough marketing assistance to insure the issue doesn't die from lack of interest.

There is another reason you must obtain a firm that is completely qualified to handle your underwriting, and one that you can rely on in complete confidence. Many of the negotiations regarding the offering will be handled *orally,* on a *handshake* basis.

Of course, this is advisable only if you are working with someone you can completely trust. If possible, it is good to check with other companies similar to yours which have gone public and obtain any information you can from their experiences with underwriters.

During registration you will be working very closely with the underwriter and will have discussions with him on a daily basis. Therefore, it is ideal if you can select an underwriter who has an office in your city. From a practical standpoint, this is often not possible and you should therefore consider the additional expense of travel and communication between the underwriter and your office.

In a small, primarily *local offering,* it is well to work with an investment firm that is familiar with your company. Again, this is sometimes not possible, particularly in tight-money periods. You must remember that the small firm is normally *regional* or completely *local* in scope; if you desire broad distribution of your stock, then you should use a firm with national connections.

However, there are distinct advantages in working with a local underwriter. Expenses will be lower due to lack of travel and communication costs. Time will be saved since you won't have to be away from the office as much. On the other hand, the prestige and ability of the local firm to sell the issue may not be such as to warrant the savings in other areas.

Of course, your prospective underwriter should have broad experience in equity financing and also have a good retail organization so that, in the event his *selling group* develops an unexpected weakness, his own organization can take up the slack and sell the issue. If yours is a *thin* or *small* issue, this will not generally be a problem, but if he has placed your stock with his own customers, he has more of an interest in sponsoring the *after market* of the stock. Finally, in this regard, the underwriter should have an excellent rapport with other securities dealers so that he will be able to organize an effective underwriting group.

A word of caution: don't shop around for the *best deal.* The word will spread that you are shopping and the prospective underwriters will not be anxious to spend the necessary time and effort

to investigate and evaluate your proposal. Decide to whom you
will make the proposal and stay with him until he renders a decision and/or offer. (See appendix C for list of underwriters
handling small issues.)

It doesn't hurt to have preliminary discussions with several
underwriters, but when you begin formulating the proposal, select
one and stick with him until a decision is reached. If the deal isn't
consummated, proceed with another. *Remember, it is unlikely
you will obtain the perfect deal; but satisfy yourself that you are
getting the best available!*

PREPARING THE PROPOSAL

Your proposal to an underwriter should include complete information on the history of your company, your current financial
situation, and the future prospects for the corporation. Following
is an outline of a typical proposal for underwriting:

I. THE COMPANY—a description of the corporation, in-
    cluding
    (a) Date of incorporation
    (b) State of incorporation
    (c) Principal stockholders
    (d) Capital structure
    (e) Locations
    (f) Customer relations

II. THE PEOPLE—a brief resume of the principal stock-
    holders, officers, directors, and key executives, including
    (a) Age
    (b) Education
    (c) Previous employment experience
    (d) Employment contracts and compensation, if any

III. THE PRODUCT—description of the product line, including
     sales volume per item, and any major sales contracts.

IV. FINANCIAL STATEMENTS—for five years, or since in-
    ception, whichever is longer.

V. THE FUTURE
    (a) Competition
    (b) Market penetration and/or saturation
    (c) Growth and profit potential

VI. THE PROPOSAL FOR A PUBLIC ISSUE
    (a) Number and type of shares to be sold
    (b) Proposed pricing of shares
    (c) Type underwriting desired

The proposal is all-important. Put your best foot forward! Be forthright and candid, but don't hesitate to dress it up either!

If you have an exclusive product, or an innovative marketing idea, *sell it*. These are the things that set you apart from others and make your proposal interesting to the underwriter.

At Donut Kastle, Inc., we came up with a distinctive building for our dealers, constructed on a modular design. We then inserted a clause in our leases allowing for *repurchase* and *removal* of the building in the event a location goes sour. This, of course, limited our liability on long-term leases, and gave our dealers a great deal of flexibility and security.

As far as I know, other franchise companies may have attempted this, but we were the only company insisting on the implementation of the program, thus setting Donut Kastle, Inc., apart from its competitors. This single item did more to help us obtain underwriting than any other factor.

Put much thought and effort into your proposal. Use pictures, graphs, charts, or anything else that will effectively tell your story.
    S E L L !

8. Methods of Underwriting

For the purposes of this discussion, we will consider two types of underwriting: *Fixed Commitment,* or *Firm Underwriting,* and *Best Efforts Underwriting.* Of the latter, there are two basic types: *Best Efforts* and *All-or-None Best Efforts.* There are other variations, but these will serve as a basis for comparison.

In *fixed commitment* or *firm underwriting,* the underwriter, together with his syndicated group of underwriters (the *selling group*), agrees to buy your stock at a fixed price. They then resell it to the public. Your price is negotiated between you and the underwriter. (In some cases, the price may be the result of competitive bidding. From a practical standpoint, however, this is not usually the case where a small company is selling its stock for the first time). The underwriter's profit is the difference or *spread* between what he pays you, the issuer, and what he resells the stock for, less commissions and expenses. Obviously, this method of underwriting is the most attractive to the issuer since it *guarantees* the sale of your stock. It is not necessarily the most common method of sale, however, and it will most probably not be the method by which the small company goes public.

Firm underwriting is usually reserved for issues in which there is demand for the stock and little chance the issue won't sell. In the event you are fortunate enough to obtain a *firm commitment,* you will receive a check for the sale, less underwriting commission, within a week after the public offering, whether or not the underwriter can resell the issue. He is obligated to buy the stock, and the subsequent resale is his responsibility.

Best Efforts Commitment—In the case of the small company, or where a stock is considered speculative, the underwriter may not agree to buy the stock. Instead, he may agree to use his *best efforts* to sell the issue on the issuer's behalf. If he doesn't sell the entire amount to the public, he has no obligation to purchase the balance. Actually, he is merely acting as your *agent,* and as such, he attempts to sell as much of the stock as possible.

In some cases, you may be advised to hold off on a public offering if you can obtain only a *best efforts* basis. However, if you have reasonable need for the capital and can put it to work, and you feel that your stock can be sold, then a *best efforts* offering is acceptable. To do this, you must have a competent and reputable underwriter who will indeed use his *best efforts* to sell the stock.

As mentioned above, there are variations of *best efforts* underwriting. In some cases, the underwriter may agree to purchase part of the issue on a firm basis, and agree to sell the balance of the issue on a strictly *best efforts* basis. This is generally called a *Combined effort.*

In some instances, the underwriters will sell an issue on an *All-or-None* basis. If they cannot sell the entire issue, the underwriting will not become effective and the purchase money will be returned to those persons who have bought stock. In other words, *all* of the stock must be sold, or *none* will be sold. This is sometimes called a *Best Efforts, All-or-None* basis.

In a case I am familiar with, the underwriting was on a "66⅔ percent, Best Efforts" basis. The underwriter and the issuer agreed that of the 150,000 shares to be offered, the offering would be effective if as many as 100,000 (66⅔ percent) of the shares were sold. Thereafter, the 50,000 shares would be sold on a strictly "best efforts" basis. The offering would be effective whether or not they were sold. In actuality, 130,000 shares were sold.

There is one additional method of underwriting that should be mentioned. It is called *Stand-by* underwriting. The issuer extends to its existing stockholders *rights* to subscribe to an additional issue at a specified price per share, within a specified time. In the event some of these rights are not exercised (which is often the case), the underwriter agrees to *Stand-by* and purchase, for resale, those securities not bought by the existing stockholders under the *rights.*

Untested companies generally must accept the *best efforts* underwriting arrangement. Therefore, they have no assurance that the entire issue will be sold. Although this method is usually used by small companies attempting to go public for the first time, it is also used at times by larger companies with excellent reputations which anticipate no trouble in selling their shares, regardless of the underwriting method. Usually, they can get better terms from the underwriter on a *best efforts* basis than they might obtain through a firm commitment.

One advantage of the *All-or-None, Best Efforts* offering is that it puts a great deal of pressure on the underwriter to complete the offering by selling all shares. He certainly does not want to cancel the entire transaction and lose all commissions he has already earned. Even though this pressure is present, he still has no firm obligation to continue the attempt to sell the shares under this method.

In summary, the small company will usually end up with a variation of the *best efforts* method of underwriting. Don't despair! If you have a worthwhile story to tell, and a good underwriter, your offering can be successful.

9. The Underwriting Agreement

As a rule, you will not enter into a written underwriting agreement until a day or so before the stock is to be sold to the public. In some cases, the contract is not signed until the very day the stock is sold. You will recall we stated earlier that the reputation of your underwriter is paramount since much of the negotiations will be done on an oral basis prior to the time the underwriting agreement is entered into. Up until the time the underwriting agreement is signed, you actually have an informal understanding between your company and your underwriter, a *gentlemen's agreement,* if you will. And until the formal agreement is signed and executed, the parties are not legally bound. However, it is rare when an underwriter will back out of an informal agreement in the absence of some drastic change in the condition of the company. But there is another factor to consider when selecting an underwriter and that is the *underwriter's financial stability.* I am familiar with at least one case where the underwriter voluntarily suspended operations on the very day an offering was to have become *effective.* Imagine the shock the issuer felt!

Usually, however, there is some writing or memorandum of the general agreement between the parties. This may be a simple outline or may be a formal *letter of intent.* Such a letter will set forth the basic agreement as to financing, the approximate offering price of the stock, and the approximate commissions. It will be signed by both parties, but there will be no *legal* obligation, only a *moral* obligation. (See Appendix A.)

Among other things, the underwriting agreement will include the following information (see Appendix B for a sample of a complete underwriting agreement):

49

1. offering price of the stock
2. commissions, discounts and expense allowances
3. method of underwriting
4. requirement of a registration statement
5. opinion of counsel and no change
6. warranties of the company
7. covenants of the company
8. indemnification agreement
9. the agreement of the company to offer the stock
10. substitution of underwriters, if necessary
11. closing

Just as in the buying or selling of real estate, a *closing* is held after the registration statement is effective and the securities have been sold. The securities are delivered to the underwriter, and the monies from the sale of stock are paid to the issuer. This is when the final paperwork is completed.

At the closing, opinions of counsel for the issuer and underwriter will be exchanged. A *comfort letter* by the accountants and officers of the issuer will be delivered, stating there has been no material, adverse changes in the status of the company.

Since the underwriting agreement will deal with expense allowances and commissions of the underwriting, it is appropriate to discuss the *cost of going public* at this point.

The underwriting commission will usually range between 6 and 10 percent of the offering price on common stock, but this is only part of the cost. In addition, the issuer usually bears the cost of preparing the registration statement and offering circular, as well as legal and accounting expenses, and the cost of Blue Sky qualifications in the various states. You can expect your expenses to run from $15,000 to $50,000, depending on the difficulty of the offering.

In a recent survey of ten small companies going public, the average offering was $575,000 and the average estimated expenses by each company was $31,000. These offerings varied from a low of $400,000 to a high of $1,000,000 and the expenses ranged from a low of $14,500 to a high of $60,000. You can readily see the variation in the expenses of these offerings. The expenses of underwriting a new stock issue are accounting fees, printing costs, federal stamp taxes, transfer fees, registrar fees, SEC registration fees, Blue Sky registration fees, travel expenses, and other miscellaneous expenses, in addition to commissions and discounts to the underwriter.

In addition, if a finder is involved in the underwriting, then the finder's fee is an additional expense usually born by the issuer. This expense item is disclosed in the underwriting agreement, made public for all to see.

10. Transfer Agent and Registrar Requirements

As an unlisted, *over-the-counter company,* you may perform your own duties as stock transfer and registration agent. You aren't required to appoint an independent registrar and transfer agent. You may, in fact, maintain your own stockholder's certificate ledger and transfer journals showing day-by-day transfers. This function will be under the jurisdiction of the corporate secretary, who will be responsible for original issue of the stock, re-issues of certificates, and conversion of certificates into other denominations. However, you will probably decide to appoint an independent transfer agent and a registrar.

Now that you are publicly owned, you will probably have a great number of stockholders, and it is likely there will be many shares changing hands daily. This is particularly true if your underwriter and his group are making a market in your stock as they should be. Don't underestimate the administrative burden this activity may be. There is no room for error in handling transfers of stock since such mistakes are often the basis for claims against the company. Because of this, it is desirable to appoint independent agencies for this function. From a practical standpoint, your agreement with the underwriter will probably require independent agents.

For the purpose of this book, there is no need to delve into the details of transferring and registering stock ownership. We simply note that the transfer agent is responsible for transferring ownership of the shares from one person to another, while the registrar is responsible for insuring that the number of shares issued does not exceed the number of those surrendered for cancellation.

In other words, the registrar insures there will not be an over-issue of the stock. He is not responsible for a valid transfer of the stock, but he does keep a record of *shares outstanding, canceled shares, and lost and destroyed shares.* He will maintain an exact record of the stock outstanding on any given day.

The same corporation may serve as transfer agent and registrar. Many times, however, each function is performed by a separate agent.

11. Marketing the Issue

The marketing of new securities is almost always accompanied by a number of complications. Obviously, the underwriter wants to complete the sale of the stock as quickly as possible, more particularly if it is a guaranteed underwriting. Usually, he will have arranged for publicity on the effective date of the offering. There will be *press releases* and *tombstone ads*. A *tombstone ad* is simply an ad in the financial newspapers and selected local newspapers that identifies the issue, gives the price and tells where the prospectus or offering circular may be obtained. Generally, the underwriter will bear the expense of these ads.

STABILIZATION

On the initial sale of your stock to the public there will always be some traders who buy shares with the intention of getting a fast rise and then dumping the stock. Of course, this will bring selling pressure to bear on the issue, and your underwriter will try to limit the number of persons buying for this purpose. At times, this has a depressing effect on the price of the stock, and under some conditions the price could fall below the initial public offering price.

To *stabilize* the market, and prevent a catastrophic decline in the market price, the principal underwriter may enter bids to buy stock offered by those wishing to sell in the early stages of the offering. It is important to understand that stabilization cannot legally occur at a price above the bid price (this would create *artificial market support*), and in any event, it cannot occur at a price above that at which the securities were originally distributed. This is actually a form of *managing* the marketing of the stock.

Because of this *managed-market* problem, the SEC requires filing of detailed reports on all stabilizing efforts.

If your underwriter has agreed to *stabilize* the market for your stock, a statement similar to the following must appear in bold type in your prospectus:

IN CONNECTION WITH THIS OFFERING, THE UNDERWRITER MAY OVERALLOT OR EFFECT TRANSACTIONS WHICH STABILIZE OR MAINTAIN THE MARKET PRICE OF THE COMMON STOCK OF THE COMPANY AT LEVELS ABOVE THOSE WHICH MIGHT OTHERWISE PREVAIL IN THE OPEN MARKET. SUCH TRANSACTIONS MAY BE EFFECTED IN THE OVER-THE-COUNTER MARKET OR OTHERWISE; SUCH STABILIZING, IF COMMENCED, MAY BE DISCONTINUED AT ANY TIME. THERE IS PRESENTLY NO MARKET FOR THE COMMON STOCK OF THE COMPANY.

ASSISTING IN THE SALE

You, as an executive of the issuer, are limited as to what assistance you can render in the sale of the securities. No doubt you will be urged to help in various ways; many will be acceptable, some unacceptable. It will behoove you to consult with your attorneys before taking any such action.

Likewise, there are definite limitations established by the SEC as to what statements the company may issue during the registration and initial sale of the stock. Certain activities of the company must be curtailed (e.g., merger or acquisition negotiations), and any material change in the status of the company must be reported. By all means, don't take chances with your registration before checking with counsel for advice.

12. After It's Over!

When you receive that call or letter telling you the issue's been sold (hopefully *oversubscribed*!), settle back in your chair, sigh a breath of relief, and *savor* the moment! *Relax*—you deserve it. *Then take the rest of the day off;* the work has just begun!

Seriously, it will be a great relief knowing the stock has been sold and that the money will be forthcoming in short order. However, with that new money will come added responsibilities that you should be prepared for. Remember the *advantages* we discussed in Chapter 1? Forget them now; they're behind you. Now come the *disadvantages*!

YOUR NEW STOCKHOLDERS

Now that you are a public company, you will have many more stockholders than previously. It follows that you should maintain a strong stockholder-relations program with these new owners and other interested persons. You should develop an organized procedure for keeping them aware of new developments, appointments, etc. You will want to furnish them with interesting, attractive annual reports, or brochures and material regarding your corporate activities.

A good beginning is to send a *letter of welcome* to the new stockholders when they first purchase their stock in the company. This establishes a rapport between the company, you as the manager, and the stockholders. If your business is that of supplying a consumer product, then of course, such a program can result in the development of new customers.

Even though you may have appointed an independent registrar who will keep accurate records of stockholders, you should also keep such a record in your office. Each day you will receive, from your registrar, a list of persons selling stock and of those purchasing stock. Some buyers will have their stock registered in *street name,* and therefore only the brokers' name will appear on the daily list.

An alphabetical card file should be established, with a card for each stockholder. Although this file need not be totally accurate, it can be of immense help from a practical standpoint whenever you receive inquiries from stockholders.

Obviously, you should answer such inquiries immediately and as thoroughly as possible. Your stockholders should receive the same treatment as your customers do, and the stockholder-relations program should receive great emphasis in your overall public relations program.

REPORTS

Periodically, you will be required to issue reports to your stockholders. These may be the regular annual or quarterly reports of your business activity or they may be special reports of changes, appointments, or other developments. Such may even help the price of your stock by encouraging your stockholders to hold their shares rather than sell them.

Of course, it goes without saying that all such reports must be correct and factual. You'll find yourself in deep trouble if you issue erroneous information just to boost your relations (or *stock?*) with your stockholders.

In addition, you will receive requests from many brokerage firms and other interested persons (libraries, etc.) to be placed on your mailing list for these reports. This doesn't hurt at all, and you should maintain such a list for these timely reports. Make it an automatic function, however, or you'll soon find you won't have time for personal attention to inquiries.

PUBLICITY

No doubt you will be interviewed by various representatives of the media and invited to speak before different groups. Generally speaking, these requests will be for general information about you and your company's activities.

Of course, you should use extreme caution in making statements, etc., during registration and immediately following the public sale of stock in order to avoid violating SEC rules. It is a good idea to consult with your attorneys as to the advisability of certain statements during this period.

MARKET FLUCTUATIONS

Watching the market in your own stock will become a fascinating game. No doubt, you will own a great number of shares, and a minor change in the price may result in a huge paper *profit* or *loss* for you. (Remember, if your stock is *lettered* or *restricted,* a paper profit is all you're likely to get for awhile!)

You'll soon find that any utterance, *positive* or *negative,* is likely to affect the price of your stock. These sensitive reactions will soon teach you the wisdom of using caution in your public statements! Nevertheless, you'll still get a thrill when you wake up one morning and find your stock went up a dollar the day before and *you made a cool $100,000 as a result!*

THE FUTURE

Now it's time to get to work and make sure all those projections you gave the underwriter come true. Now there's even more pressure for performance, and you'll be keenly aware of the effect any act or failure to act may have on your new constituency!

If the future is indeed as good as you said it would be, there may be a glorious future ahead. I hope so; *you deserve it!*

Glossary

After Market—The period immediately following initial distribution of a public offering, at which time the shares begin trading, and there are no new shares being offered.

All-or-None—An underwriting agreement whereby the underwriter agrees to use his *best efforts* to sell the issue. An additional condition of this type of agreement is that *no sale is final unless the entire issue is sold.*

Best Efforts—An underwriting agreement in which the underwriter or investment banker agrees to use his *best efforts* to sell the shares of stock being offered. There is no guarantee on the part of the underwriter that the shares will be sold. He is acting only as the agent of the issuer in attempting to sell the shares.

Blue Sky Laws—State laws that are the basis for approval or disapproval of securities to be offered in that particular state.

Broker—A firm or individual who handles orders to buy and sell securities, and who is acting as an agent rather than a principal in handling such orders.

Broker-Dealer—A firm in the business of handling orders to buy and sell securities for members of the public. It serves a customer as a broker when it is acting in the capacity of *agent.* On the other hand, if it holds an interest in the securities being traded, it is acting as a *principal,* rather than agent, since it is acting in its own interest.

Capital Stock—Individual shares of stock representing ownership in a business.

Combined Efforts—An underwriting agreement that is actually a combination of a *firm commitment* and a *best efforts* offering. Part of the stock is sold on a *firm commitment* basis and the balance is sold on a *best efforts* basis.

Dealer—A firm or individual who handles orders to buy and sell

59

stocks and who is acting as a principal rather than as an agent in handling such orders.

Due Diligence Meeting—A meeting held at the end of the waiting period following registration at which time the prospectus and the current status of the company is reviewed.

Firm Commitment—An underwriting agreement under which the underwriter gives the issuer a *firm commitment* to buy the entire issue and then resells it at a profit; also called a *Firm Underwriting.*

Hot Issue—A security which immediately sells at a considerable premium over the public offering price.

Investment Banker—A firm primarily organized to handle new issues of stock that have not been offered to the public before; also called an *underwriter.*

Issuer—A company issuing or selling stock in a public offering.

Lettered Stock—Stock issued pursuant to a letter of investment representing that the shares are being purchased by the buyer for investment purposes and not for resale; also sometimes called *restricted stock.*

Letter of Intent—A letter from the issuer to the underwriter confirming the issuer's intent to sell a specified number of shares of stock to the public. The letter will outline, generally, the terms of the underwriting agreement and other pertinent matters to the offering, but is not binding on either party.

Listed Stock—A security that is listed on one of the stock exchanges such as the New York Stock Exchange or the American Stock Exchange.

Making a Market—Refers to attempts on the part of a broker-dealer to maintain trading activity in a particular stock. By *making a market,* he maintains a firm bid and offer price in that particular security.

Market Maker—A dealer who makes a market in a particular security.

Offering Circular—That document similar to a prospectus, which is used in offerings in which the securities are sold pursuant to an exemption under Regulation A.

Over-the-Counter (OTC)—This refers to the trading of securities other than on stock exchanges. The OTC market is one between buyer and seller, rather than the auction-type sale found on exchanges.

Prospectus—A document or brochure that discloses pertinent information regarding the issuer of the securities to be sold. It is designed to enable a prospective purchaser to reach an informed decision concerning the investment value of a new issue.

Red Herring—A preliminary prospectus circulated during the waiting period following the filing of a registration statement. It lacks certain information, such as the price at which the securities will be sold.

Registration—The administrative procedure for filing information required under the Securities Act of 1933.

Registrar—Checks the transfers of stock and insures that the number of new shares issued is the same as the number given up for cancellation. The registrar also issues certificates to new stockholders.

Restricted Stock—See *Lettered Stock.*

Rights—The right extended to present stockholders to purchase additional shares of stock on a pro-rate basis, that is, in relation the number of shares he owns bears to the total shares outstanding.

SEC—Securities and Exchange Commission.

Selling Group—A group of brokers organized by the managing underwriter of a new issue. Members of the *selling group* are committed to dispose of a certain allotment of the stock.

Spread—In a *firm commitment,* the *spread* is the difference between the price paid to the issuer by the underwriter and the price at which the underwriter is able to sell the shares of stock to the public. This is his markup or profit.

Stabilization—An agreement by the underwriter to stabilize prices during the distribution of a new issue. To do this, he may purchase securities when the market price is at or below the public offering price, but not when the price is above the public offering price.

Stand-By Commitment—An underwriting agreement under which

the issuer has offered rights to its present stockholders to purchase additional shares. The underwriter *stands by* and agrees to purchase any stock that is not purchased by the present stockholders under the rights.

Street Name—These are securities held by the broker, in the broker's name rather than the customer's name. Many customers who trade frequently elect to have their securities held in this manner to facilitate trading.

Syndicate—An underwriting group that is, in effect, a joint venture or partnership, and that is dissolved as soon as the public offering is concluded.

Thin Market—Refers to the market conditions when the numbers of shares outstanding are very few. Such a condition makes the stock subject to any slight buying or selling pressure and may cause unusual market fluctuations.

Transfer Agent—The agency that records the number of shares purchased and maintains the name of the new owner on the corporate books.

Underwriter—See *Investment Banker*.

APPENDIX A
Letter of Intent

(Sample)

ABC UNDERWRITERS, INC.
INVESTMENT BANKERS & UNDERWRITERS

June 26, 1971

XYZ Manufacturing Company, Inc.
Your Town, U.S.A.

Gentlemen:

This letter confirms our understanding with respect to a proposed public offering and sale of 60,000 shares of Common Stock of XYZ MANUFACTURING COMPANY, INC. ("the Company"), pursuant to an Offering Circular to be filed pursuant to the Securities Act of 1933, upon the following terms and conditions:

1. The Company is validly existing and in good standing under the laws of the State of Delaware, with an authorized capital of 1,000,000 shares of Common Stock, 1¢ per value, of which not more than 240,000 shares will be outstanding as of the date of the offering. The Common Stock shall have no pre-emptive or redemption rights or sinking fund provisions applicable thereto.

2. The Company, as of March 31, 1971, had a net worth of at least $200,000 and for the six (6) months ended March 31, 1971, had a net income after taxes of at least $50,000.

3. We have discussed with you a program under which there will be offered to the public through us as Underwriters on an "all or none, best efforts basis," 60,000 shares of Common

Stock after the above-mentioned Offering Circular shall have been filed and become effective at an initial public offering price of $5.00 per share less a discount to us as Underwriters equal to 10% of the public offering price, i.e., 50¢ per share.

4. The Company will promptly prepare and file an Offering Circular and exhibits in connection therewith respecting the shares to be sold by us as Underwriters as set forth above and will exercise its best efforts to cause such Offering Circular to become effective as soon as possible.

5. In addition, at the closing, the Company will sell to the Underwriters for $80.00, 8,000 Warrants evidencing the right to purchase an aggregate of 8,000 shares of the Company's Common Stock during the four-year period commencing one year after the effective date of the Offering Circular. Said Warrants shall be exercisable at a price of $5.50 per share and will contain the usual provisions to protect the holders against dilution through recapitalization, merger, stock dividends and the like.

6. Within forty-eight hours prior to the effective date of the Offering Circular, we will enter into an Underwriting Agreement effective contemporaneously with the Offering Circular in form and content satisfactory to our respective counsel, containing terms and conditions usually and customarily found in instruments of the like nature with respect to "all-or-none, best efforts" commitments and containing, among other things, the usual "market conditions" and "calamity" clauses. Said Underwriting Agreement will obligate the Company to file such documents, including any post-effective amendment to the Offering Circular, or take such other steps as may be required to permit a public offering to the Underwriter's Warrants or shares of Common Stock issuable upon the exercise thereof. The Company will defray the cost of one such filing requested by the holders of the Warrants at any time after one year after the effective date of the Offering Circular provided that any such request is made at a time when audited financial statements are available, e.g., fiscal year end, or when the Company is registering other securities

for sale thereby minimizing the cost of such registration by the Company. Thereafter the cost of any such registration will be borne by the Underwriters or other holders of the Warrants of Common Stock isued thereunder. The Underwriting Agreement will further provide that for the period of five years from the effective date of the Offering Circular the Underwriter will have the right to first refusal with respect to any public or private Company offering of its securities.

7. The Company will pay the expenses of the proposed offering, including without limitation, all fees and expenses of its counsel, all original issue and transfer taxes, SEC registration fees, printing costs and accounting fees, bank escrow charges and the cost of such Blue Sky qualifications as are reasonable requested by us. Except to the reimbursement herein provided for, we shall bear all of our expenses for advertising, traveling, postage, and legal fees in connection with the offering and shall receive a non-accountable expense allowance of $8,500.00.

8. We shall mutually agree upon the independent public accountants designated to prepare and certify the financial statements to be contained in the Offering Circular, the transfer agent of the Company and such other matters as may be relevant to the proposed public offering and the verification to our satisfaction of information heretofore and to be supplied to us.

9. You have represented to us that no person is entitled directly or indirectly to compensation from the Company or from us for services as a finder in connection with the proposed offering.

10. This memorandum is accepted by the Company as a statement of our mutual intention to effect the proposed public offering as above indicated, subject to the terms hereof, our general appraisal of the securities market, and the understanding that there shall have been no material adverse change in the financial condition or affairs of the Company between the date hereof and the effective date of the Offering Circular to be filed for proposed public offering herein described and that there shall have been no such material ad-

verse change as of the closing date hereunder. This memorandum does not constitute any commitment on the part of the Company or the Underwriters and such commitment will be undertaken only after the aforementioned Underwriting Agreement, in our customary form, with reasonable amendments, as required by the Company, shall have been executed. Should the proposed public offering fail of consummation for any reason within the control of the Company (including inaccuracies of any representation hereinabove set forth), the Company will reimburse the Underwriters for their actual and reasonable out-of-pocket expenses theretofore incurred up to, but not exceeding, the sum of $2,500 prior to the filing of the proposed Offering Circular and up to, but not exceeding the sum of $5,000, if the public offering fails of consummation after the filing of the Offering Circular.

11. It is a condition of this understanding that during the period prior to the proposed public offering the Company will conduct its business in the manner in which it is now being conducted in conformity with the reports and other information heretofore furnished by the Company and that the Company will not negotiate with any other Underwriters or other person with respect to any financing on public offering of its securities pending the completion of the financing contemplated hereby.

If the foregoing correctly sets forth our understanding, please so indicate by signing and returning the enclosed duplicate copy of this Letter of Intent.

> Very truly yours,
> A B C Underwriters, Inc.
> President

CONFIRMED & ACCEPTED:

XYZ MANUFACTURING CO.

President

APPENDIX B
Underwriting Agreement

(Sample)

July 31, 1971

ABC Underwriters, Inc.
125 Main Street
New York, New York

Gentlemen:

XYZ Manufacturing Company, Inc., a Delaware Corporation (hereinafter called the "Company"), proposes to issue and sell 60,000 shares of its capital stock with a par value of $.01 per share (hereinafter called the "Stock") and you (hereinafter called the "Underwriter") agree to effect a public offering on a "best efforts, all-or-none" basis, as exclusive agent for the Company, to sell the Stock upon the terms and conditions hereinafter stated.

1. *Representations and Warranties of the Company.* The Company represents and warrants to the Underwriter that:

(A) The Company has been duly incorporated and is validly existing as a corporation in good standing under the laws of the State of Delaware, with power and authority (corporate and other) to own its properties and conduct its business as described in the Offering Circular which is part of the notification on Form 1-A referred to in subparagraph (C) hereof.

(B) The Stock has been duly authorized and, when issued and delivered pursuant to this agreement, will be duly issued, fully paid, and non-assessable, and will conform to the description thereof in the Offering Circular contained.

(C) The Company will without delay file with the Securities

67

and Exchange Commission (hereinafter called the "Commission") a notification on Form 1-A and as a part thereof an Offering Circular for general exemption of the Stock from Registration under the Securities Act of 1933, as amended (hereinafter called the "Act") pursuant to the rules of Regulation A of the Commission promulgated thereunder. The Company will file one or more amendments to such Notification on Form 1-A if required. The term "Notification," as used herein, means such Notification on Form 1-A, including exhibits and financial statements thereto when it becomes effective. The term "Offering Circular," as used herein, means the Offering Circular included as an exhibit to the Notification and in the event of any subsequent amendment or supplement thereto also means such Offering Circular as so amended or supplemented.

(D) When the Notification shall become effective and at all times subsequent thereto up to the Closing Date, the Notification and Offering Circular will fully comply with the provisions of the Act and the rules and regulations of the Commission thereunder, and neither the Notification nor the Offering Circular will contain an untrue statement of a material fact or omit to state a material fact required to be stated therein or necessary to make the statement therein not misleading; provided that the representations and warranties in this subparagraph (D) shall not apply to statements or omissions made in reliance upon information furnished herein or in writing to the Company by or on behalf of the Underwriter.

(E) The statement of financial condition of the Company as at May 31, 1971, to be set forth in the Offering Circular will present fairly the financial condition of the Company at the date thereof, and results of operations for the period shown, all in conformity with generally accepted accounting principles consistently applied during the period involved except as specifically noted thereon.

(F) Subsequent to the respective dates as of which information is given in the Notification and Offering Circular and prior to the Closing Date, and except as contemplated in the Offering Circular, the Company has not incurred nor will it have incurred any liabilities or obligations, direct or contingent, or entered into any material transaction, not in the ordinary course of business, and there has not been and will not have been any change in the capital stock or funded debt of the Company or any material adverse change in the condition of the Company, financial or otherwise.

(G) No consent of or approval by any public board or body or administrative agency, federal or state, is necessary to authorize the issue and sale of the Stock, except that the Notification must become effective under the Act and the rules and regulations of the Commission promulgated thereunder, and there must be compliance with the securities laws of the States in which the Stock is to be sold.

2. *Employment of the Underwriter.* On the basis of the representations and warranties herein contained, but subject to the terms and conditions in this Agreement set forth:

(A) The Company employs the Underwriter as its agent, to sell the Stock for the Account of the Company. The Underwriter agrees to use its best efforts as agent, promptly after the receipt of written notice of the effective date of the Notification to sell the Stock subject to the terms, provisions and conditions in this Agreement specified. The employment hereunder shall terminate thirty days after said effective date (unless said employment period is extended in the sole discretion of the Underwriter for an additional sixty days), or the Closing Date, whichever is sooner. In no event shall the Closing Date be later than ninety days after said effective date.

(B) From the date of the commencement of the public offering to the Closing Date, all proceeds from the public sale of the Stock shall be placed by the Underwriter in escrow in a separate and special account set up for that purpose at a bank or trust company, designated by the Underwriter, in the State of New York, in accordance with an escrow agreement between the Underwriter and such bank as escrow agent.

(C) As more fully described in the Offering Circular, the Stock shall be offered to the public at a public offering price of $5.00 per share. As its compensation, the Underwriter shall be entitled to receive an underwriting commission equal to $.50 per share as set forth in the Offering Circular. On or before the Closing Date the Company will issue and deliver to the Underwriter for the sum of $80.00 warrants entitling the Underwriter to purchase 8,000 shares of the Company's capital stock in the manner specified in Paragraph 6 hereof.

3. *Public Offering.* Subject to the provisions of paragraph 2, the Underwriter agrees to make a public offering of the Stock as soon after the effective date of the Notification as in the sole judgement of the Underwriter is advisable, but not later than three business days after such Notification and Offering Circular. Such public offering may be made in the open market, through co-underwriters selected by the Underwriter and through dealers in securities selected by the Underwriter as determined by the Underwriter in its sole discretion. The Underwriter may pay such concessions out of the underwriting commissions to be received by the Underwriter for the Stock sold through such co-underwriters and dealers as it may determine.

4. *Covenants of the Company.* The Company agrees that:

(A) The Company will use its best efforts to cause the Notification to become effective and to perform all things to be done and performed by it hereunder prior to the Closing Date and to satisfy all conditions precedent to the delivery by it of the Stock to be purchased hereunder.

(B) The Company will advise the Underwriter promptly (i) when the Notification has become effective, (ii) of the issuance by the Commission of any order under the Act and the rules and regulations thereunder suspending the effectiveness of the Notification or of the institution of any proceeding for that purpose, and will use its best efforts to prevent the issuance of any such order, and to secure the prompt removal thereof if issued, and (iii) will not file any amendment or supplement to the Notification or the Offering Circular of which the Underwriter shall not previously have been advised or to which the Underwriter shall have reasonably objected in writing.

(C) If at any time when on Offering Circular relating to the Stock is required to be delivered under the Act, any event occurs as a result of which the Offering Circular would, in the judgment of the Company or in the opinion of counsel for the Underwriter, include an untrue statement of a material fact, or omit to state any material fact necessary to make the statements therein, in the light of the circumstances under which they were made, not misleading, or if is necessary, in the judgment of the Company or in the opinion of counsel, for the Underwriter to amend the Offering Circular to comply with the Act, the Company promptly will prepare and file with the Commission an amendment or supplement which will correct such statement or omission or an amendment which will effect such compliance.

(D) The Company will promptly deliver to the Underwriter, two copies of the Notification as originally filed and all amendments thereto, heretofore or hereafter made (in each case including all exhibits thereto filed therewith), signed by or on behalf of the proper officer of the Company, and including a signed copy of each consent and certificate included therein or filed as an exhibit thereto together with a copy of the Offering Circular and any amendment or supplement thereto. The Company will deliver to the Underwriter on the effective date of the Notification, and thereafter from time to time, as many copies of the final Offering Circular as the Underwriter may reasonably request for the purposes contemplated by the Act and the rules and regulations thereunder.

(E) The Company represents that, and warrants that its consolidated financial statements contained in the Offering Circular shall show a net worth of not less than $200,000 on March 31, 1971, which statement may be unaudited but prepared in accordance with accepted accounting principles consistently applied.

(F) During the period of three years hereafter, the Company will furnish to you, as soon as practicable after the end of each fiscal year, a balance sheet and statements of income and surplus of the Company as at the end of and for such year prepared by certified public accountants and all in reasonable detail and presenting fairly the financial condition of the Company at the date thereof and the results of operations for the period shown, all in conformity with generally accepted accounting principles consistently applied during the period involved; and the Company will furnish to you (i) as soon as available, a copy of each report of the Company mailed to shareholders, and (ii) from time to time, such other information and financial statements (which need not be furnished more frequently than quarter-annually) of and concerning the Company as you may reasonably request. If during such period the Company has one or more active subsidiaries, such financial statements will be on a consolidated basis to the extent that the accounts of the Company and its subsidiaries are consolidated.

5. *Conditions of the Underwriter's Obligations.* The obligations of the Underwriter shall be subject to the accuracy of the representations and warranties on the part of the Company as of the date hereof and the Closing Date, to the accuracy of the Statements of the Company's officers contained in the certificates or documents delivered to the provisions hereof, to the performance by the Company of its obligations hereunder and to the following additional conditions:

(A) The Notification shall have become effective and no order suspending the effectiveness of the Notification shall be in effect at the Closing Date and no proceedings for that purpose shall be pending before, or threatened by, the Commission on such date and the Underwriter shall have received prior to the delivery of and payment for the Stock, a certificate dated as of the Closing Date and signed by the President or a Vice President of the Company to the effect that no such order is in effect or that proceedings for such purpose are pending before, or to the knowledge of the Company threatened by, the Commission.

(B) The Underwriter shall have received the opinion of counsel for the Company in form and substance satisfactory to counsel for the Underwriter for the purpose of this agreement, dated as of the Closing Date, to the effect that:

(i) The Company has been duly incorporated and is validly existing as a corporation in good standing under the laws of Delaware with power and authority (corporate and other) to own its properties and conduct its business as described in the Offering Circular;

(ii) The Stock has been duly authorized and, when

issued and delivered pursuant to this agreement, will be duly issued, fully paid and non-assessable, and Stock conforms to the description thereof contained in the Offering Circular;

(iii) To the best of its knowledge and information, there are no contracts or other documents required to be filed as a part of the Notification other than those set forth therein or filed as exhibits thereto, and that it does not know of any proceeding instituted or threatened of a character which is required to be disclosed in the Notification other than disclosed therein;

(iv) The Stock conforms as to legal matters to the descriptions thereof contained in the Notification and Offering Circular;

(v) The Notification has become, and at the Closing Date the Notification is, effective under the Act and the rules and regulations thereunder, and to the best of its knowledge no proceedings, for an order suspending the Notification are pending or threatened under the Act;

(vi) To the best of its knowledge neither the Notification nor the Offering Circular (except for the financial statements and other financial data included therein as to which such counsel need express no opinion) contains any untrue statement of a material fact or omits to state any material fact required to be stated therein or necessary to make the statements therein not misleading in the light of the circumstances under which they were made; and

(vii) This Agreement has been duly authorized, executed and delivered by the Company and constitutes a valid and binding agreement of Company.

(C) The Underwriter shall have received a certicate, dated as of the Closing Date, signed by the President or Vice President and the Treasurer or Assistant Treasurer of the Company to the effect that:

(i) The representations and warranties of the Company in this Agreement are true and correct, and the

Company has complied with all the agreements and satisfied all the conditions on its part to be performed or satisfied at or prior to the Closing Date;

(ii) No order suspending the effectiveness of the Notification has been issued, and no proceedings for that purpose have been instituted or are pending or contemplated under the Act;

(iii) The Notification and the Offering Circular contain all statements required to be stated therein, and neither the Notification nor the Offering Circular includes any untrue statement of a material fact or omits to state any material fact required to be stated therein or necessary to make the statements therein not misleading;

(iv) The financial statements and the notes thereto contained in the Offering Circular accurately reflect the financial condition of the Company as at the dates thereof and the results of operations for the periods covered thereby;

(v) Subsequent to the respective dates as of which information is given in the Notification and the Offering Circular, and except as contemplated in the Offering Circular, the Company has not incurred any liabilities or obligations, direct or contingent, or entered into any material transaction, not in the ordinary course of business, and there has not been any material adverse change in the condition of the Company financial or otherwise; and

(vi) Subsequent to the respective dates as of which information is given in the Notification and the Offering Circular, the Company has not sustained any material loss or damage to its properties, whether or not insured.

(E) The Company shall have furnished to the Underwriter such further certificates, opinions, letters and documents as the Underwriter or its counsel shall reasonably request, including, but not limited to:

(i) Certified copies of charter documents and by-laws;

(ii) Certificates of good standing; and
(iii) State tax clearance certificates for the Company
and each of its subsidiaries;
(iv) Existing contracts, franchises and/or licenses.

All such opinions, certificates, letters, documents and contracts will be in compliance with the provisions hereof only if they are satisfactory to the Underwriter and to its counsel.

In case any of the conditions specified in this paragraph 5 shall not have been fulfilled, this Agreement may be terminated by the Underwriter upon mailing or delivering written notice thereof to the Company. Any such termination shall be without liability of any party except as otherwise provided in paragraph 8 hereof.

6. *Warrants.* 8,000 warrants are to be issued and delivered to the Underwriter when the 60,000 shares are sold and shall be exercisable at a price of $5.50 per share but they are non-exercisable and non-transferable until thirteen months after the effective date of the Notification, nor later than five (5) years after such date. Such 8,000 warrants shall be placed by the Underwriter in escrow with an independent escrow agent for a period of thirteen months after such Effective Date. At any time after thirteen months after such Effective Date, upon the written request of the Underwriter on behalf of the holders of securities representing a majority of the aggregate number of warrants then outstanding and/or shares of capital stock previously issued upon exercise of such warrants, the Company will, upon receipt of such written request, use its best efforts and promptly take such steps as in the opinion of its counsel are necessary to permit a public offering of such warrants and the shares of capital stock issued or issuable upon the exercise thereof. The Company will bear the expense of preparing and filing one Registration Statement only under the Act or one Notification on Form 1-A relating to the public offering of such warrants and shares.

7. *Payment of Expenses Relative to the Offering.* The Company will pay all expenses in connection with (A) the printing of the Notification and Offering Circular, (B) printing of stock certificates, (C) costs of registrar and transfer services, (D) Blue

Sky expenses and (E) fees of its accountants. In addition, the
Company will pay the Underwriter a non-accountable expense allowance in the amount of $8,500 for (A) the preparation, print-
ing and publishing of such notices and advertisements as may be
permitted under the Act and the rules and regulations of the Commission thereunder, (B) fee of counsel for the Underwriter, (C)
any other costs of the Underwriter in connection with this underwriting. Such expense allowance will be payable to the Underwriter only if and when the Company receives from the Underwriter on the Closing Date the proceeds of the sale of the 60,000
shares of stock as hereinabove stated.

    8. *Indemnification.* (A) The Company agrees to indemnify
and hold harmless the Underwriter and each person, if any, who
controls the Underwriter within the meaning of Section 15 of the
Securities Act against any loss, liability, claim, damages or expenses (including the reasonable cost of investigation or defending
any alleged loss, liability, claim, damages or expenses and reasonable counsel fees in connection therewith), joint or several, arising
by reason of any person acquiring any stock which may be based
upon the Act or any ruling thereunder or any other statute, or at
common law, on the ground that the Notification and Offering
Circular as from time to time amended and supplemented) includes an untrue statement of a material fact or omits to state a
material fact required to be stated therein or necessary in order to
make the statements therein not misleading, unless such statement
or omission was made in reliance upon, and in conformity with,
written information furnished to the Company in connection therewith by the Underwriter; provided however, that in no case is the
Company to be liable under the indemnity agreement contained in
this paragraph with respect to any claim made against the Underwriter or any such controlling person, as the case may be, unless
the Underwriter or any such person, as the case may be, shall
have notified the Company in writing within ten (10) days after
the summons or other first legal process giving information of the
nature of the claim shall have been served upon the Underwriter
or upon such controlling person, but faliure to notify the Company
of any such claim shall not relieve the Company from any liability

which it may have to the person by whom such action is brought otherwise than on account of its indemnity agreement contained in this paragraph. In case of such notice to the Company, the Company will be entitled to participate at its own expense in the defense, or, if it so elects, to assume the defendant of any suit brought to enforce any such liability, but if the Company elects to assume the defense such defense shall be conducted by counsel chosen by it and satisfactory to the Underwriter or controlling person or persons, defendant or defendants in the suit. In the event the Company agrees to assume the defense of any such suit and retain such counsel, the Underwriter or controlling person or persons, defendant or defendants in the suit, shall bear the fees and expenses of any additional counsel retained by them, but in case the Company does not elect to assume the defendant of any such suit, it will reimburse the Underwriter or controlling person or persons, defendant or defendants, in such suit for the reasonable fees and expenses of any counsel retained by them. The Company agrees promptly to notify the Underwriter of the commencement of any litigation or proceedings against the Company or any of the Company's officers or directors, or any of them, in connection with the issue and sale of the Stock.

(B) The Underwriter agrees to indemnify and hold harmless the Company and each of the Company's officers and directors and each person, if any, who controls the Company within the meaning of Section 15 of the Act against any loss, liability, claim, damage or expenses (including the reasonable cost of investigation or defending any alleged loss, liability claim, damages or expense and reasonable counsel fees incurred in connection therewith), joint or several, arising by reason of any person acquiring any of the Stock, which may be based upon the Securities Act or any ruling thereunder or any other statute or at common law, on the ground that the Notification or Offering Circular (or the Notification and Offering Circular as from time to time amended and supplemented) includes an untrue statement of a material fact or omits to state a material fact required to be stated therein or necessary in order to make the statements therein not misleading, in so far as any such statement or omission was made in reliance upon, and in conformity with, written information furnished to the Company in connection therewith by the Underwriter; provided, however, that in no case shall the Underwriter be liable under its indemnity agreement contained in this paragraph with respect to any claim made against the Company or any person indemnified, unless the Company or such other person, as the case may be, shall have notified the Underwriter, in writing, within ten (10) days after the summons or other first legal process giving information of the nature of the claim, shall have been served upon the Company or upon such other person, but failure to notify the Underwriter of any such claim shall not relieve it from any liability which it may have to the Company or any other person against whom such action is brought otherwise than on account of its indemnity agreement contained in this paragraph. In case of any such notice to the Underwriter, the Underwriter shall be entitled to participate at its own expense in the defense, or if it so elects, to assume the defense of any suit brought to enforce such liability, but if the Underwriter elects to assume the defense, such defense shall be conducted by counsel chosen by it and satisfactory to the Company, the Company's officers and directors, or controlling person or persons, defendent or defendants, in the suit. In the event that the Underwriter elects to assume the defense of any such suit and retains such counsel, the Company, the Company's officers and directors or controlling person or persons, defendant or defendants in the suit, shall bear the fees and expenses of any additional counsel retained by them, but in the case the Underwriter does not elect to assume the defense of any such suit, it will reimburse the Company, the Company's officers and directors or controlling person or persons, defendant or defendants, in such suit, for the reasonable fees and expenses of any counsel retained by them. The Underwriter agrees promptly to notify the Company of the commencement of any litigation or proceedings against either of them in connection with the issue and sale of the stock. The Underwriter, agrees that with respect to any controlling person of the Underwriter, there shall be no liability for indemnification or for warranty under the Securities Act of 1933, as amended, by the Company unless the right of the Underwriter to such indemnification or warranty has previously been submitted to a court of competent jurisdiction for determination as to whether the claim would be, in the circumstances, against public policy as expressed in the Securities Act and that the Company will be governed by the final adjudication for such issue.

9. *Market Out.* Any other provisions of this Agreement notwithstanding, the Underwriter shall have the right, in its absolute discretion, to terminate this Agreement, without obligation, at any time after the date hereof, with respect to all or any part of the shares to be sold hereunder, (i) in the event the Underwriter shall determine that market conditions, or the operating or financial condition of the Company, or the prospects or continued prospects of the public offering then proposed or being made, are such as to make it undesirable or inadvisable to make, or continue with, the public offering herein contemplated; (ii) in the event that the Commission or any other quasi-judicial or administrative body shall threaten, or initiate, proceedings to prevent the sale or distribution of any securities of the Company or shall take any other action to interfere with the marketing of the securities provided for hereunder, or if there shall be filed by, or against, the Company any application or petition under any bankruptcy or debtor relief law, or if the Company shall suffer any of its substantial assets to be foreclosed or levied upon; or (iii) in the event that the Company shall have failed to comply with any of the provisions of this Agreement on its part to be performed, or if any of the agreements, conditions, covenants, representations, or warranties of the Company herein contained shall not have been performed or fulfilled within the times specified.

10. *Future Offering.* The Company and all affiliates including principal shareholders thereof agree that the Underwriter shall have the right of first refusal for a period of five (5) years from the Effective Date to purchase for their accounts or to sell for the account of the Company or any such affiliate thereof any securities with respect to which the Company or any affiliate may seek a public offering or with respect to any private financing by the Company or its principal stockholders. The Company or any such affiliate thereof will consult with the Underwriter with regard to

any such offering or financing and will offer to the Underwriter the opportunity to purchase or sell any such securities or provide or arrange such financing on terms not less favorable to the Company or any affiliate thereof than it can secure elsewhere. If the Underwriter fails to accept in writing such proposal for sale or financing made by the Company or such affiliate within thirty (30) days after the mailing of a notice containing such proposal by registered mail addressed to the Underwriter, then the Underwriter shall have no further claim or right with respect to the sale or financing proposal contained in any such notice. If, thereafter, any such proposal is modified, the Company shall adopt the same procedure with respect to such modified proposal as is provided hereinabove with respect to the original proposal.

(A) The Company will make available to the Underwriter and furnish copies that the Underwriter may reasonably request, of the Company's certificate of incorporation, bylaws, minutes or meetings of the stockholders and directors, and any other corporate documents.

(B) The Company and its principal stockholders have agreed that for a period of three (3) years the Underwriter shall have the right to nominate one director of the Company.

(C) For the period of two (2) years after the Public Offering Date, the Company will furnish the Underwriter with copies of the Stockholder's daily transfer sheets and upon request of the Underwriter will furnish it with a certified copy of a list of Stockholders.

11. Notices. All communications hereunder will be in writing, and, if sent to the Underwriter shall be mailed, delivered or telegraphed and confirmed to the Underwriter at 125 Main Street, New York, New York, or if sent to the Company, shall be mailed, delivered or telegraphed and confirmed to at its principal office at 146 Palm Avenue, Your Town, U.S.A.

12. *Miscellaneous.* (A) That at the time of the offering herein, the present stockholders of the Company will have 240,000 shares of common stock issued and outstanding.

(B) The respective indemnities, agreements, representations, warranties and other statements made by the Company or its officers and by the Underwriter, in or pursuant to this Agreement, will remain in full force and effect, regardless of any investigation made by or on behalf of the Underwriter or the Company or any of its officers or directors or any controlling person, and will survive delivery of any payment for the Stock.

(C) This Agreement has been made and is solely for and shall inure only to the benefit of and be binding upon the parties hereto and the officers and directors and controlling persons referred to in Paragraph 8, and their respective successors, assigns, executors and administrators, and no other person will have any right or obligation hereunder. The terms "successors" and "assigns" as used in this Agreement shall not include a purchaser, as such, from the Underwriter of any of the Stock.

(D) This Agreement shall be governed by and construed in accordance with the laws of the State of New York.

(E) The term "Closing Date" shall be fixed by notice in writing to be given by the Underwriter to the Company and such "closing date" shall not be more than ninety (90) days after the Effective Date of the Notification. The Closing Date may be changed by agreement between the Company and the Underwriter.

Please sign and return to us the enclosed duplicate of this letter, whereupon this letter will become a binding agreement between the Underwriter and the Company in accordance with its terms.

Very truly yours,
XYZ Manufacturing Company, Inc.

By ——————————————

This Agreement is hereby
Confirmed and Accepted as
of the date first above written.
ABC Underwriters, Inc.

By ——————————————
President

APPENDIX C
Firms Handling
Small Companies

The following investment banking or underwriting firms indicate an interest in handling small companies desiring to go public for the first time. The listing of these firms does not constitute an endorsement; likewise, it does not guarantee that they will handle a particular issue. They have indicated an interest, however, by returning a questionnaire specifically designed to obtain information regarding smaller underwritings.

(1) Almstedt Brothers
425 West Market
Louisville, Kentucky
(502) 585-3264
Contact: Mr. John C. Marlowe
Exchange Membership: NYSE, ASE, MWSE
Minimum Offering: $1,000,000
Maximum Offering: $10,000,000
Size Company Preferred: $150,000 to $250,000, after taxes

(2) Consolidated Securities Corp.
P. O. Box 1328
Pompano Beach, Florida 33061
(305) 943-8300
Contact: Mr. Robert C. McClure
Exchange Member: PBWSE
Minimum Offering: $500,000
Maximum Offering: $3,000,000
Size Company Preferred: $1,000,000 net worth

(3)   Edwards & Hanly Securities, Inc.
      One Whitehall Street
      New York, New York 10004
      (212) 425-9000

Contact: Mr. Jeffrey S. Balkin
Exchange Member: NYSE, ASE, PBWSE, BSE
Minimum Offering: $1,000,000
Maximum Offering: None
Size Company Preferred: $300,000 after taxes

(4)   A. G. Edwards & Sons, Inc.
      One North Jefferson
      St. Louis, Missouri 63103
      (314) 289-3000

Contact: Ms. Judith Meador
Exchange Membership: NYSE, ASE, MWSE, NSE, and others
Minimum Offering: $2,000,000
Maximum Offering: None
Size Company Preferred: Earnings, before taxes of $500,000; net
   worth, $1,000,000 or more
Comment: Prefer industries with better-than-average growth pros-
   pects; seek well-managed companies in which management will
   remain after underwriting and desires to build company; com-
   panies with record of growth in sales and earnings

(5)   First Albany Corporation
      90 State Street
      Albany, New York
      (518) 436-9721

Contact: Mr. W. F. McLaughlin
Exchange Member: NYSE, ASE
Minimum Offering: $500,000
Maximum Offering: $10,000,000
Size Company Preferred: $2,000,000 to $5,000,000 sales
Comment: Specialize in companies located in upstate New York
   and western New England

(6)   C. W. Franklin, Inc.
      140 Broadway
      New York, New York
      (212) 952-0730
Contact: Mr. Frank Wolf
Exchange Member: None

(7)   Graybar Securities, Inc.
      720 Fifth Avenue
      New York, New York 10019
      (212) 489-0576
Contact: Mr. R. D. Viscount
Exchange Member: None
Minimum Offering: None
Maximum Offering: $1,000,000

(8)   Helfer, Broughton & Buckwalter, Incorporated
      105 Hudson Street
      New York, New York
      (212) 925-3013
Contact: Mr. Richard Helfer
Exchange Member: NYSE
Minimum Offering: $200,000
Maximum Offering: $800,000
Size Company Preferred: Start-up to two years old
Comment: Prefer companies in the medical electronics industry

(9)   Hensberry & Company
      83-36th Street
      St. Petersburg, Florida
      (813) 896-9161
Contact: Mr. R. E. Hensberry
Exchange Member: None
Minimum Offering: $250,000
Maximum Offering: $2,000,000
Size Company Preferred: Offering of $500,000

Comment: Prefer medical, etc., industries; not limited to State of Florida; specialize in Regulation A offerings

(10)   Johnson, Lane, Space, Smith and Company
        Commerce Building
        Atlanta, Georgia
        (404) 523-3692

Contact: Mr. F. E. Perry

Exchange Member: NYSE, ASE

Minimum Offering: $2,000,000

Maximum Offering: None

Size Company Preferred: $500,000 to $1,000,000 net worth; minimum $250,000

Comment: Will consider all industries; current earning trend extremely important; also handle long-term debt, debt with equity participation, mergers and acquisitions

(11)   Rotan, Mosle-Dallas Union Incorporated
        2200 Bank of the Southwest Building
        Houston, Texas 77002
        (713) 224-7661

Contact: Mr. G. C. Buck

Exchange Member: NYSE, ASE, MWSE

Minimum Offering: $1,000,000

Maximum Offering: $20,000,000

Size Company Preferred: Net worth of $10,000,000

Comment: Prefer profitable Southwestern industries

Index